Date Advent Calendar Fo

24 Days Of Temptations: A Daily Challenge To Inspire Passion, Fun, Reconnect And Experiment Together. The Only Book That Includes The Dice Games & Date Night Ideas

Hearts and Phrases Editions

Hello, we are Sofia, Martina, and Elisa, the founders of 'Hearts and Phrases Editions'. We are four friends united by a dream: to brighten your everyday life. With our products, we wish to accompany you on every adventure in life, from personal growth to magical moments as a couple. Each of our diaries, journals, or calendars is created with you in mind to enhance your every nuance. Being new to Amazon, your every feedback is essential: help us spread joy and love with a review.

INDEX

Introduction.

24 Days of Temptation": far more than an Advent calendar, it invites boundless pleasure, a sensual journey that draws you into a crescendo of emotions. Each day unveils a unique challenge, carefully crafted to increase the intensity of desire and intimacy, accompanying curious and daring couples in a dance of passion that grows by the day. Immerse yourself in super-exciting proposals and be seduced by tips designed to elevate each challenge to an unforgettable experience.

With "24 Days of Temptation," you not only embrace the enthusiasm of play but also discover a series of surprises that will take you beyond the boundaries of the eroticism you already know. Each challenge is a little masterpiece of seduction, an invitation to explore your connection with increasing ardor and imagination. Each day, from gentle caresses to bolder play, adds a new hue to your love repertoire, blending pleasure into an ever more intense and surprising palette of sensations.

In addition to the 24 fiery challenges, "24 Days of Temptation" is masterfully designed to serve as an erotic dice game as well. Flip through the pages and let chance lead you to an exciting discovery: each random opening is a plunge into the unknown, an action to take, an area to explore, a place or position to dare, and an intensity or mode to experience. The book thus becomes the director of an encounter charged with adrenaline and connection.

Play does not end with the holidays' end but takes you on a journey of sensual discoveries that transcend time, creating unforgettable moments of complicity and novelty.

Dice Game No.1

To play this game, roll the dice four times; for each roll, decide which corner of the page you will use, then randomly open the book, and you are finished.

Action die:
1. Kissing
2. Tap
3. Lick
4. Nibbling
5. Whisper
6. Caress

Die with body parts:
1. Lips
2. Ears
3. Neck
4. Breast
5. Intimate area
6. Glutes

Dice with locations or positions:
1. In the kitchen
2. In the shower
3. On the couch
4. In the bedroom
5. On the chair
6. On the table

Die with duration or intensity:
1. For 1 minute
2. Slowly
3. With passion
4. Softly
5. Forcefully
6. Surprisingly

Game With Dice No.2

In this game variation, you have to roll the die twice, the first to choose the group and the second for the position. Nothing is easier!

You can also combine the two games; the possibilities are endless!

Group 1:
Numbers: 1 and 2

Group 2:
Numbers: 3 and 4

Group 3:
Numbers: 5 and 6

December 1: Intriguing Dresses

Fashion meets passion in this challenge that kicks off your seduction journey. Get ready to transform your wardrobe into a scene of flirtation and glamour.

Here's how to enrich the experience:

- **Word Prelude:** Before you start with the outfit changes, take time to explore fantasies and desires. Ignite the mood with an intimate conversation about the hidden meaning behind each type of clothing that turns you on.
- **Personal Photographic Set:** While one parades, the other can try to be a photographer, trying to capture the essence of seduction through the lens. Create a "private gallery" with the most evocative images, always respecting each other's wishes and privacy.
- **Post-show Dialogue:** Conclude the experience by openly sharing the emotions aroused by each outfit. What surprised you? What was the most compelling element? Use this moment to appreciate the art of visual seduction and the connection that arises between you.

To spice up the challenge even more:

- **Role Play:** Incorporate role play related to the outfits chosen. For example, if one wears a formal suit, the other can respond with a personal assistant outfit, resulting in a little role play.
- **Secret Accessories:** Add unexpected accessories you don't normally use, such as surprising lingerie or a particular piece of jewelry, which will only be revealed during the show.
- **'Favorite' Challenge:** After the show, elect the "winning look" and let the wearer decide a game or condition for the evening.

December 2: The Language of Touch.

Today, the challenge is exploring the sense of touch through massage, which becomes art and communication.

Instructions:

- **Artistic Setting:** Turn the room into a relaxing oasis with soft fabrics, lighting, or candles, and arrange a background playlist that evokes tranquility or pure sensuality.
- **Be Creative:** In addition to traditional massage oils, use unexpected elements such as edible body paint or spa clays, all of which can be removed with warm water or your partner's caresses.
- **Mix Styles:** Mix classical massage techniques with movements inspired by different art forms: dance, sculpture, or painting. For example, you might "paint" your partner's body with fluid movements or "mold" his body as if it were clay, trying to release tension and stress.

- **Words are unnecessary:** While performing the massage, remain silent, trying to communicate only through touch, allowing hands and fingers to express what words do not say.
- **Finish with Art:** Finish with a shared artwork on your partner's body, using edible or temporary colors, that you can admire together before rinsing it off in a shared shower or tub.

Remember that massage is not just physical foreplay but can be a powerful tool for emotional connection and nonverbal communication between partners.

December 3: Rôle Play Revealer

From classic scenarios to daring tales, role-playing is an exercise in creativity and complicity.

Here's how to make rôle play a truly immersive experience:

- **Creative Script:** Before you begin, sit down with a relaxing drink or a good glass of wine and build your skit. Whether it is a chance meeting or a blind date, let your imagination guide you.
- **Attention to Detail:** Fully immerse yourself in your characters, down to the smallest details. Change your voice, body language, and clothing to make it more real and challenging.
- **Constructive Feedback:** At the end, share a moment of reflection. What worked? What excited you the most? Was there a particular moment you would like to relive or explore?

12

To make the challenge even more exciting:

- **Surprise Element:** Incorporate into the role-playing game a sudden element that you did not plan for. It can be an object, a piece of dialogue, or a change of scenery that comes unexpectedly and adds a dash of unpredictability.
- **Location:** Do not limit yourself to a single setting. If the situation allows, move around during rôle play, moving from room to room or venturing outside if possible and safe.
- **Silence Challenge:** Try to play a scene without speaking, communicating only through body language and gestures, thus increasing tension and intimacy without speaking.

Remember that rôle play is an opportunity to explore new dynamics in your relationship and to discover hidden desires in a safe and playful space.

December 4: Adventurous Oral Exploration

Turn your evening into a discovery of the hidden wonders of oral pleasure.

Here is how to elevate this challenge to sensual art:

- **Pleasure Map:** Begin by drawing a "map" of less explored erogenous zones. Involve the senses in discovering unexpected areas that can awaken intense sensations.
- **Symphony of Sensations:** Proceed gently, measuredly, exploring each new area with care and attention. Listen to your partner's body, letting your partner's reactions, sighs, and movements guide you.
- **Dialogue of Desire: Once you have** completed your exploration, exchange impressions and feelings. What were the most surprising discoveries? Were there any particular moments you wish to relive or explore further?

To add an extra level of excitement:

- **Temperature Games:** Use hot/cold contrast to intensify sensations. A sip of a hot drink or the use of ice can turn a kiss or a puff into a memorable experience.
- **Revenge of the Senses:** Blindfold each other for total immersion in sensation and amplify the other senses: touch, hearing, and taste.
- **Counted Time:** Set a random timer during exploration. It is time to move to a new area or change the technique when it sounds.

Remember that oral exploration is an intimate journey that can strengthen your connection and mutual understanding of your partner's desires and pleasures.

December 5: Endurance Challenge

Ignite the passion with a challenge where control is everything.

Let's see how to do it:

- **Symphony of the Senses:** Use a mosaic of stimuli- the whisper of sweet words, a feather touch on the skin, the warm breath during a close breath- to seduce and challenge your partner's resistance.
- **The Stakes:** Decide together on an attractive prize for the one or the one who demonstrates the most willpower, creating an exciting, playful competition.
- **Soft Landing:** After the sensory storm, land in an oasis of tenderness with a prolonged cuddle session, acknowledging the other's commitment and mastery in not giving in to temptation.

Foto

Foto

16

To take the challenge to a new level:

- **Sensory Surprises:** Unexpected variations in temperature or texture can be a way to test endurance. Think ice cubes or silk to graze the skin.
- **Mystery Timer:** Use a timer without the partner knowing the countdown, increasing anticipation and impatience.
- **Creative Reward:** The prize for those who resist the most can be something truly desired by the other, such as a full massage, a special dinner, or the fulfillment of a fantasy.

Remember that the real victory is in the game, the journey through desire and control. This challenge tests your ability not only to resist but also to connect deeply with your partner.

Dec. 6: Light Bondage

Immerse yourself in a light bondage session where the bonds are both physical and emotional.

Here's how to intensify the experience:

- **Communication and Consent:** First, establish boundaries, signals, and safe words, thus ensuring that both of you are on the same page.
- Bonds **that Unite: Let** bondage become an expression of mutual trust. As one allows himself to be bound, the other cares, guiding the experience with respect and care.
- **Shared Reflection:** Finally, set aside time to share your impressions, listening carefully to the feelings and thoughts this practice has elicited.

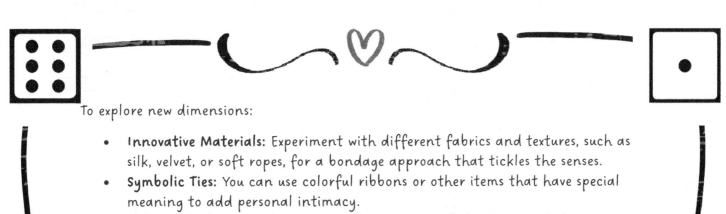

To explore new dimensions:

- **Innovative Materials:** Experiment with different fabrics and textures, such as silk, velvet, or soft ropes, for a bondage approach that tickles the senses.
- **Symbolic Ties:** You can use colorful ribbons or other items that have special meaning to add personal intimacy.
- **Enhanced After-Care:** Create an after-care ritual that may include massage, affectionate words, or a warm bath to strengthen the connection and ensure both feel loved after the experience.

Light bondage can open new doors in your intimate life, allowing you to explore the dynamics of power and vulnerability in a safe and loving space.

Dec. 7: Striptease Surprise

Revive desire with an unplanned striptease.

For a breathtaking performance:

- **Mystery Invitation:** The partner performing the striptease creates an enigmatic invitation, revealing only the time of the performance, fueling anticipation and curiosity.
- **Intriguing Plot:** Add a narrative thread or rôle play elements to the striptease, making it a compelling episode of a larger story.
- **Constructive Dialogue:** Post-performance, exchange candid feedback on what triggered the attraction most and devise variations for future performances.

For a twist:

- **Custom Music:** Choose songs that have special meaning for both of you or reflect the character you are playing.
- **Thematic Costumes:** Select outfits that are not only alluring but also related to the role or theme of the narrative for even more visual impact.
- **Ambiance: Set** the stage with dim lighting, scented candles, or decorations contributing to the atmosphere, turning the room into a private stage.
- **Creative Ending:** End the show with an unexpected element, such as an invitation for your partner to participate or a symbolic object that leads to the next chapter of your adventure.

With these details, your striptease will become an unforgettable moment of connection and exploration.

December 8: Ice Meets Fire

Experience the contrast between burning ice and caressing warmth. For an unforgettable play of sensations.

- **Solo Reconnaissance:** First, individually explore the effects of heat and cold on one's skin to learn about one's limitations and pleasures.
- **Eyes in the Dark:** Use a blindfold to shroud your partner in mystery, intensifying the jolt of each unexpected cold or warm touch.
- **Sensual Dialogue:** Post-experiment, openly share impressions, finding out what alchemy between frost and ardor ignited your passion the most.

Incorporate these elements for an exhilarating sensory experience:

- **Texture Variation:** Alternate the smooth surface of ice with the rougher surface of a hot towel to add another level of tactile stimulation.
- **Duration and Intensity:** Play with each temperature's contact duration and the intensity of heat or cold to experience different waves of pleasure.
- **Joyful End:** Close your session with a warm bath or shower together, allowing the warmth of the water to meld with the warmth of your closeness.

This game of contrasts promises to turn your December into an odyssey of sensations, creating memories that will warm you during winter nights.

December 9: Battle of the Seductions

Revisit the game of wrestling in an erotic key, turning competition into an art of courtship:

- **Honor Code:** Establish the guidelines for a passionate but always respectful challenge, clearly delineating what is allowed and what is not.
- **Arena of Love:** Prepare the battlefield with mattresses or large pillows, creating a soft, cozy space that invites close contact.
- **Conquest Reward:** Share your ideas about a reward before you begin, making sure it is attractive to both of you and adds an extra twist to your game.

For an even more stimulating experience:

- **Combat Costumes:** Wear easily removable clothing or clothing that invokes a "warrior" or "gladiator" spirit to enter the character fully.
- **Sound Atmosphere:** Create a playlist with energetic music that can give rhythm to your "battle," alternating it with sensual songs for moments of "surrender."
- **Strategic Breaks:** Insert moments when the struggle becomes mutual exploration or sensual power play.
- **After the Battle:** Treat yourself to a moment of respite after the fight, wrapping yourself in one large towel or blanket to exchange impressions and affection, nurturing the bond and complicity that such a game can intensify.

This mix of adrenaline and seduction is a sure way to rekindle desire and rediscover the pleasure of touch and physical play, taking your connection to new levels of playful intimacy.

Foto

Foto

December 10: Hidden Complicity

Turn an ordinary day into a succession of complicit glances and shared secrets, even in a crowd:

- **Secret Language:** Devise a hidden signal that can ignite a complicit smile between you, as unexpected as a whispered word or a gesture that goes unnoticed but has special meaning for you.
- **Urban Treasure Hunt:** Leave yourself notes or encrypted messages to be discovered throughout the day, suggesting spicy anticipations or bold compliments.
- **Rules of the Game:** Determine together what limits you should respect when you are in public, always maintaining respect for the context and the people around you.

25

To add an extra level of excitement:

- **Accessory Accomplice:** Carry a small object that symbolizes your game, something you can touch or discreetly display as a promise of what comes next.
- **Secret Appointments:** Arrange short "sneaky" meetings during the day, such as a coffee together or a meeting in a secluded place, to tease the imagination and anticipation.
- **Word Games:** Invent innocent dialogue that, for you, has a subtext full of innuendo, making a mundane conversation a game of deep understanding.
- **Evening Reflections:** At the end of the day, share the emotions you experienced, telling how you felt during those moments of secret play and how it affected your desire and connection.

This kind of play increases complicity and understanding, showing that intimacy is not just about touch but also about shared communication and anticipation, making the next encounter even more intense and desired.

December 11: Caressing Synesthesia

You will open the door to a world where touch reigns supreme, guiding each other's sensory journey:

- **Symphony of Sensations:** Prepare a selection of fabrics and objects with different textures. Consider interesting contrasts: the smooth coldness of a metal, the inviting softness of a cashmere, or the electricity of a rustling silk.
- **Map of Sensations:** Gently guide the objects along the blindfolded partner's body, creating sensation pathways that alternate between sweet, intense, gentle, and surprising.
- **Dialogue of the Hands:** When not using objects, let your hands talk, alternating light caresses with firmer pressure, writing invisible poetry on your partner's skin.

For an even deeper experience:

- **Ambient Music:** Accompany the exploration with music that can amplify the sensations: sounds of nature, whispered melodies, or a slow, sensual rhythm.
- **Air of Mystery:** Vary the order and choice of surprise items so the partner never knows what to expect, keeping attention and anticipation high.
- **Guide Words:** As you explore, whisper what you are doing to intensify your partner's sensory experience.

After exploration:

- **Converse:** Remove the blindfold and discuss the experience openly. Which fabrics or objects evoked the strongest reactions? Were there unexpected feelings?
- **Visual Recreation:** If your partner would agree, you could also draw or write together a "map" of the feelings you experienced, with notes on what elicited the most intense moments.

This day is dedicated to exploring the boundaries of tactile pleasure, to discover together how skin can be the canvas of art painted with caresses.

December 12: Alchemy of Essences

On this day, the art of massage becomes a ritual that unites your senses in a web of relaxation and seduction:

- **Aroma Oasis:** Turn the room into an aromatherapy sanctuary. Choose essential oils that awaken the senses or relax the spirit- lavender to soothe, ylang-ylang to energize, or sandalwood for depth.
- **Rhythm and Ritual:** Before you begin, establish a breathing rhythm together. With each exhalation, let your hands glide over your skin, joining in a shared breath that guides the movement and pressure of your hands.
- **Synergy of the Senses:** While one receives, the other gives. But the massage giver can also enjoy the experience, letting the hands feel every curve and tension in the other's body, like a dialogue without words.

Foto   Foto

For an even more immersive experience:

- **Dim lighting:** Use candles or dim lights to create an intimate atmosphere that reinforces the sense of isolation from the outside world.
- **Massage Melody:** Choose music to accompany the rhythm of your hands, a melody that can float through the air as an additional tool for relaxation.
- **Chorography of Contact:** Don't limit yourself to just the back or shoulders; carefully explore every body part. Become sculptors who shape every muscle and every tension with oil.

After the massage:

- **Shared Reflection:** Share your impressions of the experience. What sensations did the fragrances of the various oils arouse in you? How did the body respond to the different types of pressure?
- **Hydration and Care:** Drink herbal tea or a glass of water together to rehydrate the body and prolong the feeling of well-being.

This moment will be a journey into the pleasure of touch, where each caress with oil becomes a sign of affection and a promise of further discoveries in the days to come.

December 13: Burning Whispers

Today, the word becomes your most powerful tool of seduction with a game of bold dialogue that ignites the imagination:

- **Incognito of Desire:** Whether through a call or a message, assume a mysterious personality. This detachment can give you the courage to reveal hidden fantasies or play with the boundaries of the forbidden.
- **Sexy Language:** Every sentence, every term you choose, is an opportunity to challenge the norm. Speak as you never dared before, letting words be as bold as they are nuanced, in a delicate balance between said and unsaid.
- **Sensual Narration:** Don't just describe actions or desires; build a story, a context that gives depth and intensity to your game. Let the words create an atmosphere, a prelude to what might happen.

To intensify the game:

- **Voice and Silence:** Play with tone of voice and silence. A pause can be charged with anticipation; a whisper can have the effect of a shout.
- **Real-Time:** If you opt for messages, respond to each other's messages or wishes in real-time, creating a dialogue that seems to dance between the lines.

After the game:

- **Reflective Exploration:** Compare the expressive freedom you found in anonymity with your everyday freedom. Can you learn anything from this experience and bring it to your communication as a couple?
- **Fantasy and Reality:** Discuss how the fantasies you explore connect to your real desires. Is there something you would really like to experience?

On this 13th day, language becomes the vehicle for a mental sensuality that can be surprisingly powerful, opening new doors to your intimacy.

Foto

Foto

December 14: Deep Connection

This day invites you on a shared inner journey, where a calm mind and relaxed body unlock a new dimension of intimacy.

- **Synergy of Breaths:** Choose a quiet and comfortable environment. Sit back to back, close your eyes, and begin to focus on the rhythm of your breaths. Try to align them; let the breath of one become the breath of the other, creating a harmonious flow between you.
- **Meditative Touch:** During meditation, you may experience light physical contact, such as holding hands or brushing against each other's arms. This touch can be a powerful catalyst for mutual energy and presence.
- **Presence and Sensation:** Take advantage of meditation to sharpen your perception of your bodily sensations. Feel the heat generated between you, the texture of the ground or chair you are sitting on, the weight of the other's body against yours.

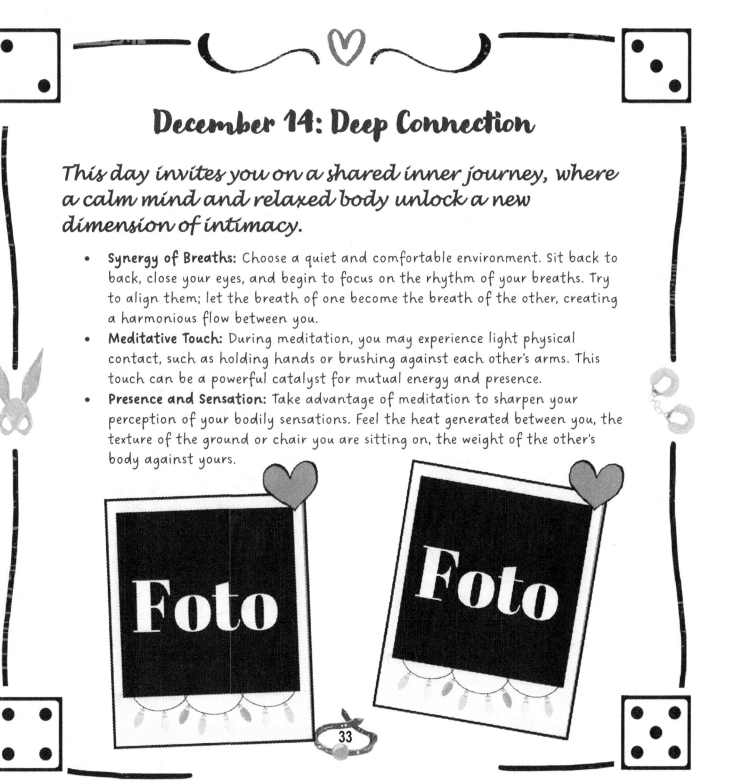

Foto Foto

33

After meditation:

- **Intimate Sharing:** Talk about what you experienced during the meditation. Was there a particular moment when you felt particularly connected? What emotions or physical sensations did you notice?
- Reflection on **Silence:** Reflect on how silence and nonverbal connection can be employed as intimacy and mutual understanding tools. Are there aspects of this experience you would like to bring into your life as a couple?

Through this sensual meditation practice, you will discover how quietness and listening can amplify your emotional and physical connection, setting the stage for an even deeper connection.

Foto

Foto

December 15: The Arsenal of Pleasure

Today, you will explore the boundaries of perseverance and lingering pleasure, diving into a multi-sensory experience dedicated to discovering new horizons of enjoyment.

- **Dream Atmosphere:** Transform the room into an oasis of serenity. Using scented candles, incense, or diffusers with essential oils can help create an atmosphere that invites tranquility and deep relaxation. The playlist should include songs that reflect peace and harmony, such as nature sounds or soft jazz melodies.

- **Pleasure Arsenal:** Gather a selection of massage tools that entice you to explore different types of stimulation. Hot stones to relax muscles, rollers to gently massage away tension, and vibrating toys to add a dimension of exciting surprise. Each tool will be an extra step in the journey of sensual discovery.

- **Connection and Attunement:** Make eye contact and nonverbal communication pillars of your intimate union during massage. You can convey affection, desire, and approval through a glance, thus encouraging deeper understanding.

After the massage:

- **Shared Reflection:** Openly share your impressions of the experience you just had. What did you discover new about your partner's pleasure? What sensations stimulated your imagination and desire the most?

- **Future Planning:** Consider what elements of this challenge you want to reincorporate into your love routine. Did you enjoy the variety of techniques and tools? Is there anything you would like to explore more deeply?

Today's goal is to immerse yourself in the art of dilated pleasure, opening yourself to a slow and meticulous exploration that will lead you together to discover new heights of shared pleasure.

December 16: The Casket of Secret Pleasures.

In the journey of "24 Days of Temptation," today is the turn of the chapter on hidden fantasies, an invitation to open up in a deeper and more vulnerable way. With the "fantasy box," you will create a space of free expression where your innermost secrets can come to life.

- **Wish Safe:** Prepare a small box and decorate it together, where everyone can deposit their hidden dreams on folded pieces of paper. There are no rules about what to write: it can be a simple word, an evocative phrase, or a short story.
- **Dialogue Without Barriers:** When you open the chest, do so in a quiet, private moment. Read the fantasies together and welcome them with curiosity and an open mind. Remember that there is no place for judgment; this is a session of discovery and acceptance.
- **Wish Fulfillment:** Choose one or more fantasies to fulfill and plan how to bring those secret confessions to life. Consider preparing an unexpected scenario for your partner and fulfill one of his fantasies when he least expects it.

After the experience:

- **Sharing and Growth:** Talk about what you have discovered about each other and yourself. How do you feel after sharing and perhaps realizing a secret fantasy?

- **Treasure of Possibilities:** Keep the box in an accessible place. It can become an ongoing resource to inspire new adventures and keep the mystery and excitement alive.

This day is dedicated to the courage to reveal and embrace one's innermost desires, the power of shared trust, and the magic of seeing a dream turn into reality.

December 17: Power Games.

In your sensual advent calendar, December 17 is the day to explore the allure of control and surrender through consensual and confident power games. It is an opportunity to lightly experience the intoxication of domination and submission.

- **Contract of Desires:** Before we begin, sit down and outline the game's rules. Who will be the Master? Who is the devoted slave? Write down your thoughts, boundaries, and safety signals. Clarity is the most powerful aphrodisiac in this game.
- **The Punishment Mosaic:** Devise together a menu of gently provocative "punishments" designed not to humiliate but to delight. These can range from reading sensual poetry aloud to performing a seductive dance to an intensely dedicated massage to each other.
- **Scales of Pleasure:** As you go into the game, always keep an eye on the scales of consent and pleasure. Roles can be fluid; each "order" is a disguised invitation to shared and expected pleasure.

After the experience:

- **Complimentary Reflections:** Conclude with an honest dialogue about how you felt. Were there moments of surprise? Aspects that were particularly exciting or that you did not find enjoyable?
- **Treasure of Emotions:** Save the "contract" and "punishment" ideas for the future. They may become permanent fixtures in your erotic repertoire or serve as inspiration for future games.

This is a day to experience alternative intimacy, play with boundaries, and discover new horizons of mutual pleasure.

December 18: Deep Pleasure.

On December 18, your sensual journey takes you into the unknown and intriguing world of anal exploration, a territory that requires trust, communication, and open curiosity. It is an opportunity to expand the boundaries of your intimacy with mutual care and respect.

- **Careful Preparation:** Begin your exploration with a conversation about expectations and fears. Inquire together about the safest and most pleasurable practices, deciding what products to use, such as specific lubricants and toys designed for this specific area.
- **Progressive Warm-up:** Beginning with caressing and massaging around the area can help relax muscles and create an atmosphere of anticipation and desire. Prolonged foreplay is essential to ensure the comfort of both.
- **Guidance and Consent:** As you explore, proceed slowly, giving and receiving constant feedback. Communication will enable you to proceed at the right pace, respecting the body's signals and your partner's desires.

After the experience:

- **Sharing and Caring:** Reserve time to discuss the experience, listening to each other's feelings and thoughts without rushing. It is also important to ensure both of you feel physically comfortable after such intimacy.
- **Intimate Reflection:** If the experience was positive, you can plan together how and when to incorporate it back into your sex life. If, however, it was not as hoped, reflect on what could be done differently in the future.

This day is an invitation to discover new horizons of pleasure in a context of complete trust and mutual understanding.

Foto

Foto

December 19: Attraction Ball

Dance, one of the oldest forms of expression, can become the nonverbal language of your desire. On December 19, let bodies speak with movements that defy gravity and seduce gracefully.

Here's how:

- **Sensory Attunement:** Choose music that vibrates the strings of desire, songs that speak to your soul as much as to your body. The right music is the first step in creating an atmosphere of anticipation.
- **Confidence in Movement:** If necessary, practice some dance steps on your own, discovering how each movement can be full of promise. It is not about performing the perfect dance but letting the body express what words do not say.
- **Tension Crescendo:** Select clothes that ignite the imagination that can be revealed piece by piece to the rhythm of the music in a game of see-saw and don't-see that can keep the partner suspended in sweet torment of anticipation.

After the Dance:

- **Open Heart Reflections:** Share the emotions aroused by dance. What movements ignited your passion? What pleasantly surprised you? Sharing strengthens the bond and prepares you for future adventures.
- **Echo of Movement:** End the evening by letting the movements of the dance transform into caresses and embraces, allowing the rhythm to continue to guide you in a symphony of intimacy.

This day invites your love to express itself in a choreography that is yours alone, unique, and unrepeatable, woven with the invisible threads of desire and complicity.

December 20: Before Indiscreet Eyes.

The art of being seen without crossing the boundaries of one's comfort zone can be a subtle dance of desire and boldness.

Here is how to structure this experience:

- **Private Boundary:** Choose a place where you have the security of privacy but simultaneously offer that thrill associated with the possibility of being discovered. This could be a secluded place outdoors at night, a hotel room with a window overlooking a view that is not too exposed, or your home with the right lighting to create striking shadows.
- **Confidence Dialogue:** Conduct a frank discussion about what "exhibitionism" means to each of you. What are the fantasies, expectations, and fears? Establishing boundaries and expectations is critical to a positive and challenging experience.
- **If the idea excites you but makes you nervous**, begin with small acts of exhibitionism, such as standing by an open window wearing less clothing than usual or hugging tenderly where you might be seen.

After Experience:

- **Reciprocal Evaluation:** After experiencing the agreed level of exhibitionism, take some time to evaluate how you feel. Was there a balance between excitement and comfort? Is there anything you would like to do differently next time?
- **Deepening Desire:** Harness residual adrenaline and arousal to guide you toward deeper and more personal intimacy. Accumulated tension can turn into fiery passion, making the sexual act that follows more intense and connective.

Exploring exhibitionism in a way that is safe, consensual, and pleasurable can open new doors of sensory and emotional perception, strengthening mutual trust and connection between you.

December 21: The Script of Desire

Advanced role-playing can be an exciting way to explore different fantasies and dynamics within the relationship.

Here are some steps to fully immerse yourself in the experience:

- **Creative Brainstorming:** Before you begin, sit down together to discuss possible scenarios. Do you want to dive into a classic teacher-student narrative or perhaps an encounter between a seductive spy and his mystery contact? Be creative and try to develop a theme that you both find intriguing.
- **Ambiance and Atmosphere: Transform the play space once you have chosen the setting.** Soft lighting, thematic decorations, and background music can transport you to another world. If your scenario calls for a 'bar,' set up a corner with bottles and glasses; if it were a 'prison,' you could set up a space simulating a jail cell.
- **Clothing and Accessories:** Costumes are an essential component of getting into character. Whether as simple as a change of clothing or adding distinctive accessories, wearing something different can help break up the every day and intensify immersion in the role.
- **Script and Improvisation:** While some prefer to have a detailed script to follow, others find that a list of key points allows for more flexibility and spontaneity. Decide together which approach you prefer and prepare accordingly. Remember that the fun is also in adapting and reacting to surprises that arise during play.

Post-game:

- **Shared Reflection:** Share your feelings about role-playing. What excited you the most? Was there a particular moment that struck you or that you found particularly engaging?
- **Constructive Feedback:** Discuss openly and without judgment what you enjoyed and what you could change. This will not only improve future role-playing sessions but can also increase intimacy between you.
- **Preserve the Spark:** If there have been particularly electrifying aspects of role-playing, think about how you might incorporate them into your sex life more regularly.

Role play can be a way to rediscover each other and explore new dimensions of your sexuality in a safe and playful environment.

December 22: New Perspectives.

Exploring new sexual positions can be an exciting adventure and a way to discover unexpected pleasures.

Here's how to meet the challenge:

- **Search and Selection:** Start by searching together for different positions. You can consult books, online guides, or even apps that provide detailed illustrations and descriptions. Choose a position that you both find challenging, and that suits your physical abilities.

- **Preparation:** Be sure to have everything you may need on hand. This might include pillows for support, lubricant, or even a chair or other furniture if the position requires outside support.

- **Communication:** Maintain open communication throughout the process. Make sure you both feel comfortable and are not afraid to say if something is wrong or uncomfortable.

- **Preliminaries:** Spend time on foreplay to make sure that both of you are sufficiently relaxed and aroused. This can make it easier and more enjoyable to try a new position.

- **Patience and Play:** Don't expect the new position to work perfectly on the first try. Laugh at any setbacks and treat the whole experience as a game. Practice makes perfect!

- **Evaluation:** After trying a new position, discuss it together. What did you enjoy about it? Was there anything that could have been done differently? Was there a particular feeling or corner that you found particularly enjoyable?

Remember that sexual exploration should always be based on mutual consent and comfort. It is important to respect the limits of your body and your partner. Although a position may seem exciting in theory, it may not be suitable for you in practice, and that's okay. The important thing is to have fun together while exploring.

Foto

Foto

December 23: Harmony of Pleasures.

A mutual exploration of masturbation can be incredibly intimate and engaging.

Here are some steps to follow for this challenge:

1. **Environment**: Create an environment that is comfortable and free of distractions. You can use soft lighting, music, or anything that helps you relax and focus on the experience.
2. **Positioning**: Sit facing each other so that you can maintain eye contact. Make sure you are close enough to touch each other if you wish.
3. **Warm-up**: Start with foreplay to get in the right mood and increase arousal.
4. **Communication**: Talk about what you like and how you like to be touched. This will help create an atmosphere of openness and trust.
5. **Rhythm**: Begin by touching each other, gradually increasing the intensity and pace. Communicate whether you want to slow down or speed up, finding a pleasant rhythm for both of you.
6. **Synchronization**: As you approach climax, try to synchronize your breathing rhythm. This can help tune your body and potentially synchronize your orgasms.
7. **Support**: If one of you feels you are about to reach orgasm before the other, you may slow down or stop for a moment to wait for the other.
8. **Appreciation**: After reaching or not reaching orgasm simultaneously, take time to cuddle and share appreciation for the shared experience.

Remember, the goal is not only to achieve orgasm together but also to enjoy the journey. The pressure of "having" to synchronize orgasms can sometimes hinder the

experience; therefore, the important thing is to remain playful and open to what happens. Intimacy and shared pleasure are the real success of this exercise.

Foto

Foto

December 24: Your Celebration

Opening gifts can become exciting and playful, intensifying intimacy and passion.

Here is how you might proceed:

1. **Careful Selection**: Choose gifts carefully based on your partner's preferences and fantasies. It can be something you have discussed or a surprise you think they might like.
2. **Festive** ambiance: Creating a festive atmosphere can amplify the excitement. Decorate the room with dim lights or candles and put sensual Christmas music in the background if you like the idea.
3. **Inviting Packaging**: Wrap gifts seductively. Use silk ribbons, luxurious packaging, or even lingerie as wrapping. The opening process becomes part of the foreplay.
4. **Presentation of Gifts**: Exchange gifts one at a time, leaving room for appreciation and experimentation with each new toy or lingerie item.

5. **Sensual Exploration**: Explore how each new item can be incorporated into your games. Show each other how you would like to use or be used with the new gift.

6. **Role-playing**: You can even create a scenario around the idea of "gifting"-for example, one of you might "gift" yourself to the other with a red ribbon tied around your body or part of it.

7. **Variation of Sensations**: If gifts include sex toys, experiment with different settings and sensations. For lingerie, experiment with touching and feeling the fabric on the skin.

8. **Appreciation**: After playing with your new gifts, spend some time reflecting on what you particularly enjoyed and how these gifts can be included in your regular sex life.

9. **Reciprocity**: Make sure you both have the opportunity to enjoy gifts and attention. Fairness in giving and receiving pleasure is important for maintaining intimacy and connection.

10. **Lasting Memories**: Consider creating a special memory of the night, whether it is a photo together (if you feel comfortable and feel it is safe), a shared journal of experiences, or even just a moment of shared gratitude.

Foto

Foto

This will be the culmination of your erotic Advent calendar and the beginning of new adventures for your sex life. Remember that communication and consent always come first in any shared experience. Have fun and happy holidays!

Conclusion

With Christmas night illuminated by twinkling lights and hearts warmed by shared closeness, the Erotic Advent calendar ends. This December journey has been an intimate and joyful exploration of the many facets of pleasure and bonding, an adventure through sensations, emotions, and connections that have enriched the fabric of your relationship.

From the first tentative and expectation-laden attempt to the final opening of the gifts, each day has been a step along a path that has made your bond stronger and deeper. You have experimented and learned, laughed and whispered, and shared meaningful silences and looks that speak more than a thousand words.

Now, as the final hours of December 24 draw to a close in a dance of desire and pleasure, there is a sense of fulfillment but also anticipation. Every end hides a new beginning, and this calendar's end is the beginning of future adventures. The discoveries are not meant to be confined to these winter days but to flourish in the days and months to come.

You have woven together a carpet of memories that will remain under your feet as you move forward in your story. The Advent calendar will be a reminder that curiosity and affection can create magic in the little things and that sharing yourself is the most precious of gifts.

And so, under the silent night sky and with hearts filled with what has been shared, you can smile at each other, knowing that the true meaning of this calendar was not just in the acts of pleasure but in the journey made together, hand in hand, with the courage to explore and the love to guide you.

Happy Christmas, and may the joy of these days accompany you in every step and every touch for all the days to come.

Printed in Great Britain
by Amazon

31840196R00033